## Touching The Classics
## 译点经典

重庆市外事侨务办公室 ◎ 编

当代世界出版社

图书在版编目（CIP）数据

译点经典：英汉对照／重庆市外事侨务办公室编.
—北京：当代世界出版社，2011.1
ISBN 978-7-5090-0451-7

Ⅰ.①译… Ⅱ.①重… Ⅲ.①英语—汉语—对照读物
Ⅳ.①H319.4

中国版本图书馆 CIP 数据核字（2011）第 006592 号

| 书　　　名： | 译点经典 |
|---|---|
| 出版发行： | 当代世界出版社 |
| 地　　　址： | 北京市复兴路 4 号（100860） |
| 网　　　址： | http://www.worldpress.com.cn |
| 编务电话： | (010) 83908400 |
| 发行电话： | (010) 83908410（传真） |
| | (010) 83908408 |
| | (010) 83908409 |
| | (010) 83908423（邮购） |
| 经　　　销： | 新华书店 |
| 印　　　刷： | 北京才智印刷厂 |
| 开　　　本： | 880 毫米×1230 毫米　1/32 |
| 印　　　张： | 4.5 |
| 字　　　数： | 85 千字 |
| 版　　　次： | 2011 年 1 月第 1 版 |
| 印　　　次： | 2011 年 1 月第 1 次 |
| 印　　　数： | 20000 册 |
| 书　　　号： | ISBN 978-7-5090-0451-7 |
| 定　　　价： | 10.00 元 |

如发现印装质量问题，请与承印厂联系调换。
版权所有，翻印必究；未经许可，不得转载！

# 序

**黄奇帆**

当今的世界正发生着日新月异的变化，在这个全球化的时代，只有具备国际化视野，善于利用东西方差异带来的机会才能更好的谋求发展。

重庆，正处于建设国际化大都市过程中的经济快速发展期，要建设国际化大都市就要有国际化视野，就是要立足重庆，从战略的高度，把我们的视野从内陆跨越边界、跨越海洋，投放到全球化的大背景下，以国际化作为我们城市发展的主导方向，从而确立重庆建设国际化大都市的定位和目标。

重庆的市民要成为具备国际化视野的人才，就要让我们头脑里的思想观念、意识、价值取向来一次新的解放，新的转变，新的提升，让我们的视野、心胸达到"会当凌绝顶，一览众山小"那样

的高度和广度，那样的气度和开放度。市民们在思维方式、工作态度、精神状态等方面，都应该树立国际意识，具备建设国际化大都市的气魄。

　　脚步再快，都不可能比目光更快更远。而读书则是广泛吸收国外知识文化精华的捷径。重庆人每年读的书平均是4.5本，新加坡人每年要读8.3本，日本人要读18本，而美国人则多达25本。从读书时间上讲，重庆人每周平均读书2.5小时，新加坡人5.9小时，日本人8.8小时，美国人14.4小时。看来啊，一个地方的生活节奏越快，经济越发达，国际化程度越高，人们越是需要读书，喜欢读书。

　　如果说《读点经典》已经为我们开了一个好头，要想汲取更多外国文化精髓的话，那就从这本《译点经典》开始吧！

# 目  录
## Contents

序／黄奇帆　1

外国名言警句选　1

外国诗词歌曲选　47

外国散文小说节选　77

外国影视戏剧作品节选　99

跋 可给人些许启迪的书／李肇星　130

# 外国名言警句选

1. Life is like a sea. Only can a strong-willed person reach the opposite shore.

——Karl Marx

生活就像海洋，只有意志坚强的人，才能到达彼岸。

作者：卡尔·马克思（德 1818~1883），德国政治哲学家及社会理论家，马克思主义创始人。

2. There is no royal road to science, and only those who do not dread the fatiguing climb of its steep paths have a chance of gaining its luminous summits.

——Karl Marx

在科学上面没有平坦的大道，只有不畏劳苦沿着陡峭的山路攀登的人，才有希望达以光辉的顶点。

作者：卡尔·马克思

3. It is not the consciousness of men that

determines their being, but, on the contrary, their social being that determines their consciousness.

———Karl Marx

不是意识决定存在,而是社会存在决定意识。

作者:卡尔·马克思

4. An ounce of action is worth a ton of theory.

———Friedrich Engels

一盎司的行动顶得上一吨的理论。

作者:弗里德里希·恩格斯(德 1820~1895),马克思主义者,是马克思主义的创始人卡尔·马克思的挚友,《共产党宣言》起草者之一。在马克思逝世后,帮助马克思完成了《资本论》等著作,并且领导国际工人运动。

5. Without a revolutionary theory there can

be no revolutionary movement.

——Lenin

没有革命的理论,就不会有革命的运动。

作者:列宁(俄 1870~1924),格弗拉基米尔·伊里奇·乌里扬诺夫,列宁是他参加革命后的化名。列宁是伟大的马克思主义者、革命家、政治家、理论家、布尔什维克党创立者、苏联建立者。他发展了马克思主义,形成了列宁主义理论。马克思列宁主义者称他为"全世界无产阶级和劳动人民的伟大导师和领袖"。

6. A man can fail many times, but he isn't a failure until he begins to blame somebody else.

—— J. Burroughs

一个人可以失败多次,但是只要他没有开始责怪旁人,他还不是一个失败者。

作者：巴勒斯（美 1837~1921），美国散文家，美国环保运动中的重要人物，影响深远的生态学家。代表作有《醒来的森林》、《鸟与诗人》、《清新的野外》和《清新的原野冬日的阳光》等。

7. All that you do, do with your might; things done by halves are never done right.

—— R. H. Stoddard

做一切事都应尽力而为，半途而废永远不行。

作者：理查德·亨利·拖达德（美 1825~1903），诗人。

8. Dare and the world always yields①. If it beats you sometimes, dare it again and again and it will succumb②.

—— W. M. Thackeray

---

① yield：v. 屈服，让步，投降。
② succumb：v. 屈服，屈从；听任；弃置（常与 to 连用）。e.g.：Most of us are known to succumb to persuasion through the media.
我们之中的大多数人都抵挡不住传播媒介的宣传。

大胆挑战，世界总会让步。如果有时候你被它打败了，不断地挑战，它总会屈服的。

作者：萨克雷（英 1811～1863），英国 19 世纪著名的批判现实主义作家。他的作品主题鲜明，时常批判英国维多利亚时期上流社会没落贵族和资产阶级暴发户等各色人物的丑恶嘴脸和弱肉强食、尔虞我诈的人际关系。代表作有《名利场》、《巴利·林顿的遭遇》等。

9. Few things are impossible in themselves; and it is often for want① of will, rather than of means, that man fails to succeed.

—— La Rocheforcauld

事情很少有根本做不成的；其之所以做不成，与其说是条件不够，不如说是决心不够。

---

① want n. 在这里作"缺乏"讲，而 means 是金钱、财富、财产、资力的意思，fail to do sth. 未能做成某事。

作者：罗切福考尔德（法 1613~1680）

10. Genius only means hard-working all one's life.

—— Mendeleyev

天才只意味着终身不懈地努力。

作者：门捷列耶夫（俄 1834~1907），俄国化学家，曾发明元素周期律。

11. Great works are performed not by strength, but by perseverance①.

—— Samuel Johnson

完成伟大的事业不在于力量，而在于坚韧不拔的毅力。

---

① persevere：v. 坚持，孜孜不倦，不屈不挠；perseverant：adj. 能坚持的；perseverance：n. 坚持，坚韧不拔，不屈不挠。

作者：塞缪尔·约翰逊（英 1709~1784），英国 18 世纪著名的诗人、散文家、传记家。他编撰的《英语大词典》和《莎士比亚全集》对英语的传播、英国文学的发展和正确认识莎士比亚做出了巨大贡献。生长在严肃的古典主义（严格讲究诗歌、戏剧创作规范）氛围下，约翰逊却对文学创作持开放态度。

12. If you have great talents, industry① will improve them; if you have but② moderate③ abilities, industry will supply their deficiency④.

—— Joshuas Reynolds

如果你很有天赋，勤勉会使其更加完善；如果你能力一般，勤勉会补足其

---

① industry：n. 勤劳，勤奋，孜孜不倦；industrious：adj. 勤勉的，勤劳的，勤奋的。

② have but：仅有，只有。

③ moderate：adj. 适度的，稳健的，温和的，中等的。

④ deficiency：n. 缺乏，不足；deficient：adj. 不足的，不充分的，有缺陷的。

缺陷。

作者：乔舒亚·雷诺兹（美 1723～1792），散文家。

13. It is enterprise① which builds and improves the world's possessions. Thrift may be the handmaid and nurse of enterprise. But equally she may not. For the engine which drives enterprise is not thrift②, but profit.

—— John Maynard Keynes

进取心造就和增加了世界上的财富。节俭可能是进取心的仆人的护理人，同样也可能不是。因为进取心的动力不是

---

① enterprise：n. 本义为事业，企业。这里引申为事业心、进取心、冒险精神、开拓精神、首创精神、独创性。其形容词形式为 enterprising，义为有事业的、有胆量的、富于想象力的。

② thrift：n. 节俭，节约；thrifty 为其形容词形式。

节俭，而是利润。

作者：约翰·梅纳德·凯恩斯（英 1883~1946），英国经济学家，因开创了所谓经济学的"凯恩斯革命"而称著于世。其代表作《就业、利息和货币通论》（The General Theory of Employment, Interest and Money, 简称《通论》）强调贸易差额对国民收入的影响，相信保护政策如果能带来贸易顺差，必将有利于提高投资水平和扩大就业，最终导致经济繁荣。

14. When an end is lawful and obligatory[①], the indispensable[②] means to it are also lawful and obligatory.

—— Abraham Lincoln

如果一个目的是正当而必须实现的，则达到这个目的的必要手段也是正当而

---

① obligatory：adj. 义不容辞的，义务的，必须的，其名词形式为 obligation，作义务讲。另有一个衍生短语：be (feel) obliged to do sth. 不得不做某事。

② indispensable：adj. 不可缺少的。

必须采取的。

作者：亚伯拉罕·林肯（美 1809~1865），美国第 16 任总统。1862 年 9 月 22 日，林肯宣布了他亲自起草的具有伟大历史意义的文献——《解放黑奴宣言》草案（即后来的《解放宣言》），美国黑人从此获得解放。林肯是饱含热情的杰出演讲家，有着优秀的民主自由作风，而且还是道德的楷模。他毕生致力于国家的统一和民族的稳定，他独特的精神力量和伟大的人格使他在美国国民心中的威望甚高。

15. The only limit to our realization of tomorrow will be our doubts of today.

—— Franklin Roosevelt

实现明天理想的唯一障碍是今天的疑虑。

作者：富来克林·罗斯福（美 1882~1945），美国第 32 任总统。他因领导美国在第二次世界大战中获胜，被称为"赢得战争的总统"。他也成功地解决了美国 30 年代经济危机。罗斯福三次连任美国总统，1944年他再次获胜，成为美国历史上唯一连续四次当选的总统。

16. If you wish to succeed, you should use persistence① as your good friend, experience as your reference, and prudence as your brother and hope as your sentry.

—— Thomas Edison

如果你希望成功，当以恒心为良友、以经验为参谋、以谨慎为兄弟、以希望为哨兵。

作者：托马斯·爱迪生（美 1847~1931），美国著名发明家。最重要的发明是电灯、同步电报机、改良电话机、留声机和复印机。

17. Don't part with your illusions, when

---

① persistence：n. 坚持，固执；其形容词形式为 persistent。

they are gone, you may still exist, but you have ceased to live.

—— Mark Twain

不要放弃你的幻想,没有幻想你仍能生存,但虽生犹死。

作者:马克·吐温(美 1835~1910),美国批判现实主义文学的奠基人,世界著名的短篇小说大师。他经历了美国从"自由"资本主义到帝国主义的发展过程,其思想和创作也随之变化。他擅长使用幽默、讽刺和方言写作,针砭时弊,一针见血,毫不留情,其创作将现实主义的刻画和浪漫主义的抒情和谐地统一。其代表作品有《汤姆·索耶历险记》、《哈克贝利·费恩历险记》、《镀金时代》、《王子与贫儿》及《败坏了哈德莱堡的人》等,被誉为"美国文学界的林肯"。

18. A man is not old as long as he is seeking something. A man is not old until regrets take the place of dreams.

—— J. Barrymore

只要一个人还有所追求,他就没有老。直到后悔取代了梦想,一个人才算老。

作者:巴里穆尔(美 1847~1905),演员。原名赫伯特·布莱恩,在伦敦首演舞台剧后,于1875年迁居纽约,取巴里穆尔为艺名。

19. A spectre is haunting Europe-the spectre of communism. All the powers of old Europe have entered into a holy alliance to exorcise this spectre: Pope and Tsar, Metternich and Guizot, French Radicals and German police-spies.

Where is the party in opposition that has not been decried as communistic by its opponents in power? Where is the opposition that has not hurled back the branding reproach of communism, against the more advanced opposition parties, as well as against its reactionary adversaries?

Two things result from this fact:

I. Communism is already acknowledged by all European powers to be itself a power.

II. It is high time that Communists should openly, in the face of the whole world, publish their views, their aims, their tendencies, and meet this nursery tale of the spectre of communism with a manifesto of the party itself.

To this end, Communists of various nationalities have assembled in London and sketched the following manifesto, to be published in the English, French, German, Italian, Flemish and Danish languages.

一个幽灵,共产主义的幽灵,在欧洲徘徊。旧欧洲的一切势力,教皇和沙皇、梅特涅和基佐、法国的激进党人和德国的警察,都为驱除这个幽灵而结成了神圣同盟。

有哪一个反对党不被它的当政的敌人骂为共产党呢?又有哪一个反对党不拿共产主义这个罪名去回敬更进步的反对党人和自己的反动敌人呢?

从这一事实中可以得出两个结论：

共产主义已经被欧洲的一切势力公认为一种势力；

现在是共产党人向全世界公开说明自己的观点、自己的目的、自己的意图并且拿党自己的宣言来对抗关于共产主义幽灵的神话的时候了。

为了这个目的，各国共产党人集会于伦敦，拟定了如下的宣言，用英文、法文、德文、意大利文、佛来米文和丹麦文公布于世。

作者：马克思、恩格斯
出处：《共产党宣言》


20. Ignorance is the curse of God, knowledge is the wing wherewith we fly to heaven.
—— William Shakespeare

无知乃是罪恶，知识乃是我们藉以飞向天堂的翅膀。

作者：威廉·莎士比亚（英 1564~1616）

出处：《亨利六世》第二卷，第四幕，第七场（Henry VI, Part 2, Act IV, Scene VII）。《亨利六世》共有三卷。这三部曲通过一个软弱无能的国王为国家带来的灾难向观众提出了关于国家命运和前途的重大问题：王权问题。在这三部曲中人物性格是鲜明的：亨利六世心慈面软，像个活菩萨；作为国王，他是软弱无能的，不能解决矛盾。因此，当约克公爵理查举兵反叛时，他无力制止，终于导致了英国的内战，即长达30年之久的红白玫瑰战争（1455~1485）。

21. Rich gifts wax poor when givers prove unkind.

—— William Shakespeare

如果送礼的人不是出于真心，再贵重的礼物也会失去它的价值。

作者：莎士比亚（英 1564~1616）

出处：《哈姆雷特》第三幕，第一场（Hamlet, Act III, Scene I）。《哈姆雷特》创作于1602年，主要讲述丹麦王子哈姆雷特为父报仇的故事。本剧的精彩点在于莎翁将哈姆雷特的犹豫和忧郁个性刻画得入木三分。这一场正是哈姆雷特考虑是否要杀死叔父的时候。

## 22. Virtue is bold, and goodness never fearful.

—— William Shakespeare

### 美德行天下，善良永无敌。

作者：莎士比亚（英 1564~1616）

出处：《一报还一报》，第三幕，第一场（Measure for Measure, Act III, Scene I）。《一报还一报》（亦译为《量罪记》）改编自一部意大利悲剧《普洛莫斯和卡桑德拉》，不过，莎士比亚将这个故事安排了一个喜剧的结尾。故事是说维也纳的一个少年绅士克劳狄奥，因为与女友未婚先孕，被本城摄政安哲鲁判处死刑。克劳狄奥的姐姐依莎贝拉去向摄政求情，被摄政要求做其情妇才可赦免克劳狄奥。幸好有出外微服私访的本城公爵在暗中调度，让被摄政拒婚、摄政原来的未婚妻顶替依莎贝拉去和摄政幽会；又安排将另一个死囚处死，顶替下克劳狄奥。最后，公爵公开出场，判决摄政安哲鲁必须娶前未婚妻，克劳狄奥才幸免于难，与已经怀孕的女友完婚。

23. What's in a name? That which we call a rose by any other name would smell as sweet.

—— William Shakespeare

名称有什么关系呢？玫瑰不叫玫瑰，依然芳香如故。

作者：莎士比亚（英 1564~1616）

出处：《罗密欧与朱丽叶》，第二幕，第二场（Romeo and Juliet, Act II, Scene II）。凯普莱特和蒙太古这两大家族有宿仇。蒙太古家的儿子罗密欧和凯普莱特家的女儿朱丽叶相爱。两人秘密结婚后，罗密欧却在和朱丽叶的堂兄提伯尔特的决斗中将对方杀死，政府下令驱逐罗密欧。罗密欧刚刚离开，出生高贵的帕里斯伯爵就来向朱丽叶求婚。凯普莱特命令朱丽叶下星期四就结婚。朱丽叶去找神父想办法，神父给了她一种药，服下去后就像死了一样，但四十二小时后就会苏醒过来。神父答应她派人找回罗密欧，挖开墓穴，让她和罗密欧远走高飞。朱丽叶依计行事。可是，罗密欧在神父的送信人到来之前就已经听说朱丽叶死亡的消息。他在半夜来到朱丽叶的墓穴旁，杀死了阻拦他的帕里斯伯爵，掘开了墓穴，掏出毒药一饮而尽。等朱丽叶醒来见到死去的罗密欧，也不想独活人间，遂拔剑自刎。两家的父母从神父口中得知儿女情深，从此消除积怨，并在城中为罗密欧和朱丽叶铸了一座金像。

## 24. Smooth runs the water where the brook is deep.

—— William Shakespeare

静水流深。

作者：莎士比亚（英 1564~1616）

出处：《亨利六世》第二卷，第三幕，第一场（Henry VI, Part 2, Act III, Scene I）。这一幕是玛格莱特王后、波福红衣主教、萨福克和约克公爵在亨利王面前一起诬陷葛罗斯特爵爷的情景。王后诋毁葛罗斯特爵爷目中无人，红衣主教诽谤爵爷草菅人命，约克公爵无中生有地控诉爵爷横征暴敛、收刮民财。尽管爵爷指出这四人各怀鬼胎，都有篡夺王位的野心，但昏庸无能的亨利六世经不起一席人

的软磨硬泡，最终妥协将忠心耿耿的葛罗斯特爵爷关押入狱。萨克福的这句"静水流深"流传甚广，即河床越深，河面越平静。这里，萨克福指葛罗斯特爵爷图谋造反已久，却装出一副老实相。

## 25. There is a history in all men's lives.
## —— William Shakespeare

### 所有人的生活里都有一部历史。

作者：莎士比亚（英 1564~1616）

出处：《亨利四世》下篇，第三幕，第一场（Henry IV, Part 2, Act III, Scene I）。《亨利四世》(1597) 是莎士比亚历史剧的代表作。书名为《亨利四世》，实际上描写其在位时期，亨利王子（就是后来的"亨利五世"）的活动。

## 26. Sweet are the uses of adversity[①].
## —— William Shakespeare

---

① adverse：adj. 不利的；adversity：n. 不幸，灾难。

苦尽甘来。

作者：莎士比亚（英 1564~1616）

出处：《皆大欢喜》第二幕，第一场（As You Like It, Act II, Scene I）。这句话是西尼尔（Senior）公爵在被自己的兄弟篡权并驱赶出宫后的感悟。

句中的"uses"可当"profits"理解，即在逆境中的"收获"。


27. Do not, for one repulse①, forgo the purpose that you resolved to effort.
—— William Shakespeare

不要只因一次挫败，就放弃你原来决心想达到的目的。

作者：莎士比亚（英 1564~1616）

---

① repulse n. 击退，拒绝。

28. It is not enough to help the feeble① up, but to support him after.

—— William Shakespeare

仅仅把弱者扶起来是不够的，还要在他站起来之后支持他。

作者：莎士比亚（英 1564~1616）

出处：《雅典的泰门》，第一幕，第一场（Timon of Athens, Act I, Scene I）。《雅典的泰门》是莎士比亚的最后一部悲剧，大约写于1607~1608年。雅典富有的贵族泰门慷慨好施，但不善交友，贫穷或富有的朋友们都骗取其钱财，使其负债累累。之后，"朋友们"与其断绝了往来，泰门在冷漠的俗世的折磨下，想办法请来以前虚情假意的"朋友"，他愤怒地用热水浇在这些人身上，然后离开了不能忍受的城市，躲进洞穴，茹毛饮血，终惨死在绝望中。

29. Truth needs no colour; beauty, no

---

① the feeble 意为"意志弱的人"；又如：the strong，强大的人；常用复合词 feeble-minded 表"低能的"意思。

pencil.

—— William Shakespeare

**真理不需色彩，美丽不需涂饰。**

*作者*：莎士比亚（英 1564~1616）

*出处*：《十四行诗》，第 101 首（The Sonnets, 101）。整首诗鼓舞诗人要大胆用华丽辞藻歌颂美，不要认为修饰是做作的表现。原文如下：

O truant Muse, what shall be thy amends

For thy neglect of truth in beauty dyed?

Both truth and beauty on my love depends;

So dost thou too, and therein dignified.

Make answer, Muse: wilt thou not haply say

Truth needs no colour, with his colour fixed;

Beauty no pencil, beauty's truth to lay;

But best is best, if never intermixed?

Because he needs no praise, wilt thou be dumb?

Excuse not silence so; for't lies in thee

To make him much outlive a gilded tomb,

And to be praised of ages yet to be.

Then do thy office, Muse; I teach thee how

To make him seem long hence as he shows now.

偷懒的诗神呵，你将怎样补救

你对那被美渲染的真的怠慢？

真和美都与我的爱相依相守；

你也一样，要倚靠她才得通显。

说吧，诗神；你或许会这样回答：

"真的固定色彩不必用色彩绘；

美也不用翰墨把美的真容画；

用不着搀杂，完美永远是完美。"

难道她不需要赞美，你就不作声？

别替缄默辩护，因为你有力量

使她比镀金的坟墓更享遐龄，

并在未来的年代永受人赞扬。

当仁不让吧，诗神，我要教你怎样

使她今后和现在一样受景仰。

注：诗神，此处指代诗人。

30. Take honour from me and my life is undone.

—— William Shakespeare

吾誉若失，吾生休已。

作者：莎士比亚（英 1564~1616）

31. If you would go up high, then use your own legs! Do not let yourselves be carried aloft[①]; do not seat yourselves on other people's backs and heads.

—— F. W. Nietzsche

如果你想走到高处，就使用自己的两条腿！不要让别人把你捧得太高；更不要骑在别人的背上和头上。

作者：弗里德里希·威廉·尼采（德1844~1900），哲学家，他的著作对宗教、道德、现代文化、哲学以及科学等领域提出了广泛的批判和讨论。他的写作风格独特，经常使用格言和悖论的技巧。尼采对于后代哲学的发展影响极大，尤其是对存在主义与后现代主义的影响。代表作有《悲剧的诞生》等。

出处：《苏鲁支语录》（The Spake Zarathustra）。"超人"和"自强个体"是《苏鲁支语录》的主题。

---

① aloft：adv. 在高处，在上。

32. Man errs so long as he strives.

—— Goethe

人若进取就必有舛误。

作者：歌德（德 1749~1832）。作为诗人、自然科学家、文艺理论家和政治人物，歌德是魏玛共和国时期古典主义最著名的代表；而作为诗歌、戏剧和散文作品的创作者，他是德国最伟大的作家之一，也是世界文学领域的一个出类拔萃的光辉人物。代表作有《少年维特的烦恼》、《浮士德》等。

出处：《浮士德》第一卷，"天堂开场白"（Faust: a tragedy. Part 1. Prologue in Heaven）。这句话是上帝所说。

33. Only those who have the patience to do simple things perfectly ever acquire the skill to do difficult things easily.

—— Friedrich Schiller

只有耐心做好简单工作的人，才能轻松完成困难的事。

作者：弗里德里希·席勒（德 1759~1805），18世纪著名诗人、哲学家、历史学家和剧作家，德国启蒙文学的代表人物之一。席勒是德国文学史上著名的"狂飙突进运动"的代表人物，歌德的挚友，死后和歌德葬在一起。代表作有《阴谋与爱情》等，《阴谋与爱情》是"狂飙突进运动"最杰出的成果，此剧揭露了上层统治阶级的腐败生活与宫廷中尔虞我诈的行径，直接质问当时的德国社会严格的等级制度，具有乌托邦色彩。后期创作风格转变为古典主义，早年的浪漫激情接近消失。著名的诗集作品有《欢乐颂》、《理想》等。

34. Ordinary people merely think how they shall spend their time; a man of talent tries to use it.

——Arthur Schopenhauer

普通人只想到如何度过时光，有才能的人设法利用时间。

作者：亚瑟·叔本华（德 1788~1860），德国哲学家。他继承了康德对于现象和物自体之间的区分。不同于他同代的费希特、谢林、黑格尔等

取消物自体的做法,他坚持物自体,并认为它可以通过直观而被认识,将其确定为意志,认为意志独立于时间、空间,所有理性、知识都从属于它,人们只有在审美的沉思时才能逃离其中。叔本华将他著名的极端悲观主义和此学说联系在一起,认为意志的支配最终只能导致虚无和痛苦。他对心灵屈从于器官、欲望和冲动的压抑、扭曲的理解预言了精神分析学和心理学。他文笔流畅优美,思路清晰。代表作有《作为意向和表象的世界》等。

出处:《生活的智慧》,第二章:"人性"(The Wisdom of Life, Chapter II, Personality, or What a Man is)。

35. The decline of literature indicates the decline of a nation; the two keep in their downward tendency.

—— Goethe

文学的衰落表明一个民族的衰落。这两者一起走着下坡路。

作者:歌德(德 1749~1832)

出处：《歌德关于世界、人性、文学、科学和艺术的观点》（Coethe's opinions on the world, mankind, literature, science and art, translated by Otto Wenckstern）。

36. Drinking Kimchi-water first before eating Ddeok.

急功近利。

出处：韩国谚语。Kimchi-water 是"韩国泡菜汤"，Ddeok 是"年糕"。这句话字面意思是喝了泡菜汤才吃年糕。在韩国，一般是吃完年糕后主人才上泡菜汤，意在淡口，或者补充水分。而这样颠倒顺序比喻急于求成或不切实际的愿望。

37. I prefer the tumult[①]of liberty to the quiet of servitude[②].
—— Thomas Jefferson

① tumult：n. 骚动，拥挤。
② servitude：n. 苦役，奴隶状态。

我愿自由而有危险,不愿安宁而受奴役。

作者:托马斯·杰弗逊(美 1801~1809),美国第三任总统,也是美国独立宣言(1776年)主要起草人,是美国开国元勋中最具影响力者之一。其任期中的重大事件包括路易斯安娜购地案(Louisiana Purchase)、1807年禁运法案(Embargo Act of 1807)以及路易斯与克拉克探勘(Lewis and Clark Expedition)。他创立并领导的民主共和党(Democratic-Republican Party),成为今日民主党之前身。

出处:"托马斯·杰弗逊1787年1月30日给美国第四任总统詹姆斯·麦迪逊的一封信"(Thomas Jefferson to James Madison, January 30, 1787)。

38. Ideal is the beacon. Without ideal, there is no secure direction; without direction, there is no life.

—— Leo Tolstoy

理想是指路明灯。没有理想,就没有

坚定的方向；没有方向，就没有生活。

作者：列夫·托尔斯泰（俄 1828~1910），19世纪末20世纪初俄国最伟大的文学家，也是世界文学史上最杰出的作家之一。代表作有长篇小说《战争与和平》、《安娜·卡列尼娜》、《复活》以及自传体小说三部曲《童年》、《少年》、《青年》。他的成就登上了当时欧洲批判现实主义文学的高峰。他被列宁称颂为具有"最清醒的现实主义"的"天才艺术家"。被公认为全世界的文学泰斗和"俄国革命的镜子"。

39. The strongest of all warriors[①] are these two — time and patience.

—— Leo Tolstoy

最强大的战士有二：时间和耐心。

作者：列夫·托尔斯泰（俄 1828~1910）

---

① warrior：n. 勇士，战士。

40. It is the tears of the earth that keep her smiles in bloom.

—— Rabindranath Tagore

是大地的泪点,使她的微笑保持着青春不谢。

作者:罗宾德拉纳特·泰戈尔(印度 1861~1941),著名诗人、文学家、作家、艺术家、社会活动家、哲学家和印度民族主义者。1913 年他凭借宗教抒情诗《吉檀迦利》(Gitanjaei,即《牲之颂》)获得诺贝尔文学奖,是首位获得诺贝尔文学奖的印度人(也是首位获此殊荣的亚洲人)。他与黎巴嫩诗人纪·哈·纪伯伦齐名,并称为"站在东西方文化桥梁的两位巨人"。他的作品反映了印度人民在帝国主义和封建种姓制度压迫下要求改变自己命运的强烈愿望和他们不屈不挠的反抗斗争,充满了鲜明的爱国主义和民主主义精神,同时又富有民族风格和民族特色。其重要诗作有诗集《故事诗集》、《新月集》、《飞鸟集》、《流萤集》、《园丁集》、《边缘集》、《生辰集》等。

出处:《飞鸟集》

41. Life finds its wealth by the claims of the world, and its worth by the claims of love.

—— Rabindranath Tagore

生命从世界得到财富,从爱情得到价值。

作者:罗宾德拉纳特·泰戈尔(印度 1861~1941)

出处:《飞鸟集》

42. Man only likes to count his troubles, but he does not count his joys.

—— Fyodor Dostoevsky

人们总是记住烦恼,忽视快乐。

作者:费奥多尔·陀思妥耶夫斯基(俄 1821~1881),19世纪群星灿烂的俄国文坛上一颗耀眼的明星。"托尔斯泰代表了俄罗斯文学的广度,陀思妥耶夫斯基则代表了俄罗斯文学的深度"。代表作

《罪与罚》。陀思妥耶夫斯基是心理描写和善恶矛盾性格组合的专家，他对人类肉体与精神痛苦的震撼人心的描写是其他作家难以企及的。他的小说戏剧性强，情节发展快——接踵而来的灾难性事件往往伴随心理斗争和痛苦的精神危机，他以此揭露各种人物关系的纷繁复杂、矛盾重重和深刻的悲剧性。

## 43. Silly critics are not as visible as silly praisings.

—— Alexander Pushkin

愚蠢的批评没有愚蠢的赞扬那么明显。

作者：亚历山大·普希金（俄 1799~1837），著名的文学家、伟大的诗人、小说家，现代俄国文学的创始人。19世纪俄国浪漫主义文学主要代表，同时也是现实主义文学的奠基人、现代标准俄语的创始人，被誉为"俄国文学之父"、"俄国诗歌的太阳"。他诸体皆擅，创立了俄国民族文学和文学语言，在诗歌、小说、戏剧及至童话等各个文学领域都给俄罗斯文学提供了典范。被高尔基誉为"一切开端的开端"。普希金作品歌颂自由、光明、理智，他"用语言把人们的心灵燃亮"。

44. They say to me, "Would you know yourself, you would know all men." And I say, "only when I seek all men shall I know myself."

—— Kahlil Gibran

他们告诉我：如果你了解自己，你就会了解全人类。我说：只有当我追求全人类，我才能真正了解我自己。

作者：纪·哈·纪伯伦（黎巴嫩 1883~1931），诗人、作家、画家。被称为"艺术天才"、"黎巴嫩文坛骄子"，是阿拉伯现代小说、艺术和散文的主要奠基人，和泰戈尔一样都是近代东方文学走向世界的先驱。著有散文诗集《泪与笑》、《先知》、《沙与沫》等。纪伯伦作品多以"爱"和"美"为主题，通过大胆的想象和象征的手法，表达深沉的感情和远大的理想。思想受尼采哲学影响较大，作品常常流露出愤世嫉俗的态度或表现某种神秘的力量。是阿拉伯近代文学史上第一个使用散文诗体的作家。他是位热爱祖国、热爱全人类的艺术家。

45. If the other person injures you, you may forget the injury; but if you injure him you will always remember.

—— Kahlil Gibran

如果他人伤害你，你可以忘记它。

但如果你伤害别人，你必将永远记住它。

作者：纪·哈·纪伯伦（黎巴嫩 1883~1931）

46. Live as if you were to die tomorrow. Learn as if you were to live forever.

—— Mohandas Karamchand Gandhi

要像明天就会死亡一样地活着，像会永远活着一样地学习。

作者：莫罕达斯·甘地（印度 1869~1948），

尊称圣雄甘地，印度民族主义运动和国大党领袖。他的"非暴力不合作"的主张，影响了全世界的民族主义者和那些争取和平变革的国际运动。通过"非暴力"的公民运动，甘地使印度摆脱了英国的统治，激发了其他殖民地的人们起来为他们的独立而奋斗。甘地的主要信念是"satyagraha"，英语译成"truth force"，意为"真理的力量"、"追求真理"等。这鼓舞了其他的民主运动人士，如马丁·路德·金、曼德拉等人。

47. To see the universal and all-pervading[①] spirit of truth face to face one must be able to love the meanest[②] of creatures as oneself.

—— Mohandas Karamchand Gandhi

真理的精神遍布各地、处处皆有。但若想面对它，必须像爱护自己那样爱护地位最低微的人。

---

① pervade：v. 弥漫，遍及，漫延。
② mean：adj. 低劣的，卑贱的，平均的。

作者：莫罕达斯·甘地（印度 1869~1948）

48. I have not the shadow of a doubt that any man or woman can achieve what I have, if he or she would make the same effort and cultivate the same hope and faith.

—— Mohandas Karamchand Gandhi

任何人只要作出和我一样的努力，胸怀同样的期望和信心，就都能做到我所做到的一切。对此，我是确信无疑的。

作者：莫罕达斯·甘地（印度 1869~1948）

49. Whenever I despair①, I remember that the way of truth and love has always won. There may be tyrants② and

---

① despair: v. 绝望，失望，丧失信心（常与 of 连用）；作名词时，常与 in 搭配，in despair。
② tyrant: n. 暴君。

murderers, and for a time, they may seem invincible①, but in the end, they always fail. Think of it: always...

—— Mohandas Karamchand Gandhi

每当我绝望时，我会铭记，只有真理和爱能得胜。暴君和凶手也许能逞凶一时，但不能横行一世。仔细想一想，永远如此……

作者：莫罕达斯·甘地（印度 1869~1948）

50. We come nearest to the great when we are great to humility②.

—— Rabindranath Tagore

当我们甚为谦卑的时候，便是我们最接近伟大的时候。

---

① invincible: adj. 不可征服的，难以制服的。
② humility n. 谦卑，谦逊。

作者：罗宾德拉纳特·泰戈尔（印度 1861～1941）

## 51. Self-conceit may lead to self-destruction.

—— Socrates

**自大者将自毁。**

作者：苏格拉底（古希腊 公元前469～公元前399），著名的哲学家，被后人广泛视为西方哲学的奠基者。他的哲学思想主要体现在以下几个方面：

心灵的转向，把哲学从研究自然转向研究自我，即后来人们所常说的，将哲学从天上拉回到人间。

灵魂不灭说，苏格拉底明确地将灵魂看成是与物质有本质不同的精神实体。这一学说将精神和物质明确对立起来，成为西方哲学史上唯心主义哲学的奠基。

苏格拉底反诘法（Socratic irony）是西方哲学史上最早的辩证法。

## 52. It is a great art to do the right thing in the right season.

—— Socrates

在适当的时候做适当的事是一门伟大的艺术。

作者：苏格拉底（古希腊 公元前469~公元前399）

53. I count him braver who overcomes his desires than him who conquers his enemies; for the hardest victory is the victory over self.
—— Aristotle

我认为克服自己欲望的人比征服敌人的人更勇敢；因为最难获得的胜利是战胜自己。

作者：亚里士多德（古希腊 公元前384~前322年），世界古代史上最伟大的哲学家、科学家和教育家之一。是柏拉图的学生，亚历山大的老师。马克思曾称亚里士多德是古希腊哲学家中最博学的人，恩格斯称他是古代的黑格尔。亚里士多德一生勤奋治学，从事的学术研究涉及到逻辑

学、修辞学、物理学、生物学、教育学、心理学、政治学、经济学、美学等，写下了大量的著作，他的著作是古代的百科全书，据说有四百到一千部，主要有《工具论》、《形而上学》、《物理学》、《伦理学》、《政治学》、《诗学》等。他的思想对人类产生了深远的影响。他创立了形式逻辑学，丰富和发展了哲学的各个分支学科，对科学做出了巨大的贡献。

54. Time is the most fair and reasonable —— it never gives more to anyone. To hard workers, time leaves clusters of fruits while to the lazy, time only grey hair and empty hands.

—— Gorkey

时间是最公平合理的，它从不多给任何人什么。时间馈赠勤劳者的是一串串果实；时间给懒惰者的是缕缕白发和空空的双手。

作者：高尔基（俄 1868~1936），前苏联伟大的无产阶级作家、社会活动家，社会主义现实主义文学的奠基人。他出身贫苦,亲身经历了资本主义残酷的剥削与压迫,这对他的思想和创作发展具有了重要影响。登上文坛后,他塑造了一系列工人和无产阶级革命者的英雄形象,抨击了西方资本主义制度和反动思潮。代表作有《海燕之歌》,自传体三部曲《童年》、《在人间》、《我的大学》等。

55. One coin in the money-box makes noise than when it is full.

存钱桶里只有一个铜板时,比里头装满了硬币还要响。

出处:阿拉伯格言

56. Thinking well is wise, planning well, wiser, doing well wisest and best of all.

思考缜密,聪明;计划周密,更聪明;执行彻底,最聪明最完善。

出处:伊朗格言

# 外国诗词歌曲选

## 1. WHAT IS SUCCESS

What is success?

To laugh often and love much;

To win the respect of intelligent people,

And the affection of children;

To earn the approbation① of honest critics,

And endure the betrayal② of false③ friends;

To appreciate beauty;

To find the best in others;

To give oneself;

To leave the world a little better,

Whether by a healthy child,

A garden patch,

Or a redeemed④ social condition;

To have played and laughed with

---

① approbation: n. 认可,嘉许。
② betrayal: n. 背叛,叛变;叛卖,出卖;其动词为 betray。
③ false: adj. 不忠诚的,不忠实的。
④ redeem: v. 补救;改善;在此处译为"改善社会条件"。

enthusiasm,

And sung with exultation①;

To know even one life has breathed easier,

Because you have lived...

This is to have succeeded.

—— Ralph Waldo Emerson

## 成功的内涵

成功是什么？

笑口常开，爱心永在，

赢得智者的尊重，

孩子们的爱戴；

博得真诚的认可，

容忍损友的背叛；

欣赏美好的东西，

发现别人的可爱。

学会无私地奉献，

给世界增添光彩：

要么培育出健康的孩子，

要么留下花园一块，

---

① exultation：n. 狂喜，大悦，欢欣。

亦或是改善社会条件；

尽情娱乐、笑得畅快，

把欢乐的歌唱起来；

甚至知道一个生命活得自在，

因为你的一路走来……

这就是成功的内涵。

作者：拉尔夫·沃尔多·爱默生（美 1803～1882）

背景：拉尔夫·沃尔多·爱默生是美国 19 世纪著名的浪漫主义散文家之一。他是"超验主义"（Transcentalism）的创始人。

超验思想虽然以基督教思想和清教思想为其内核，但却是结合各种哲学思想，包括新柏拉图主义、德国理想主义甚至某些东方神秘思想的一个集大成的世界认知方式。超验主义者提倡个性解放，鼓吹打破神学和外国教条主义的束缚，给浪漫主义以新的血液。这也是美国浪漫主义独有的特点。爱默生的代表作有《论自然》（On Nature）、《自力更生》（Self-reliance）等。

## 2. RESULTS AND ROSES

The man who wants a garden fair,

Or small or very big,

With flowers growing here and there,

Must bend his back and dig.

The things are mighty few on earth,

That wishes can attain,

Whatever we want of any worth,

We've got to work to gain.

It matters not what goal you seek,

Its secret here reposes①:

You've got to dig from week to week,

To get results or roses.

—— Edgar Albert Guest

## 硕果和玫瑰

要想有个美丽花园,

面积大小姑且不管,

只要园中长满鲜花,

就必须把汗水挥洒。

有愿望就能实现,

这样的事还真是少见,

---

① repose: n. 休息,睡眠,静止; v. 休息,依靠,信赖。

只要想要的东西有价值,

就得靠努力去创造。

目标是什么并不重要,

秘诀终归只有一条:

周而复始不怕劳累,

才能收获硕果或者玫瑰。

作者:埃德加·阿尔贝特·格斯特(美1881~1959),诗人。

3. ON WINGS OF SONG

On wings of song,

My darling, I carry you off,

Off to the fields of the Ganges[①];

I know the loveliest spot there.

A red-blossoming garden lies there

In the silent moonlight;

The lotus flowers are waiting

For their beloved sister.

---

① Ganges: n. 恒河(印度北部与孟加拉国境内的河流,发源于喜马拉雅山,注入孟加拉湾)。

The violets① giggle and caress,

And look up at the stars;

Secretly the roses whisper

Fragrant tales in each other's ear.

Pious, wise gazelles②

Hop over and listen;

And in the distance is the roar

Of the holy river's waters.

There we shall sink down

Beneath the palm tree,

Imbibing love and calm

And dreaming a blissful dream.

—— Christian Johann Heinrich Heine

## 乘着歌声的翅膀

乘着歌声的翅膀,

心爱的人,我带你飞翔,

向着恒河的原野,

那里有最美的地方。

一座红花盛开的花园,

---

① violet: n. 紫罗兰。
② gazelle: n. 小羚羊。

笼罩着寂静的月光,
莲花在那儿等待
它们亲密的姑娘。
紫罗兰轻笑调情,
抬头向星星仰望;
玫瑰花把芬芳的童话
偷偷地在耳边谈讲。
跳过来暗地里倾听
是虔诚聪颖的羚羊;
在远的地方喧腾着
圣洁的河水的波浪。
我们要在那里躺下,
在那棕榈树的下边,
吮吸爱情和寂静,
沉入幸福的梦幻。

作者:克里斯蒂安·约翰·海因里希·海涅（德 1797~1856）

背景:海涅是 19 世纪最重要的德国浪漫主义诗人、新闻工作者、讽刺性杂文作家和论战者之一。他使日常语言诗意化,将报刊上的文艺专栏和游记提升为一种艺术形式,赋予了德语一种全新的风格上的轻松与优雅。他是诗作被翻译得最

多的德国诗人之一。海涅最广为人知的就是这首由门德尔松为之作曲的通过音乐传播的《乘着歌声的翅膀》。

## 4. AZALEAS

If you would go,

Tired of me,

Nothing will I say.

I shall pick azaleas

At Yaksan, Yungbyun,

And deck the path you tread.

Tread gently

On my azaleas

Where the path is decked.

If you would go,

Tired of me,

No cry shall you hear of mine.

—— Kim, So-wol

### 金达莱花

假如因厌烦而离开我,

我将

默默地送你一程。
摘来
宁边药山的一束金达莱,
铺满了你去的路上。
请你
以轻盈的脚步,
走过花瓣之路。
假如因厌烦而离开我,
我将
不会有一滴泪水。

**作者**：金素月（朝鲜 1903~1935）

**背景**：金素月是朝鲜著名诗人，朝鲜现代诗歌的奠基人之一。他的诗继承了朝鲜古典诗歌和民谣的传统，具有独特的民族艺术风格和浓厚的乡土气息。他善于写自然景色和农村风光，笔法细腻，语言朴素，不事雕琢，从对一山一水、一草一木的描写中，流露出爱国的深情。《金达莱花》是他的代表作之一，产生于20世纪20年代，描写了那个时代的真实婚姻、感情生活。金达莱是朝鲜的国花，象征希望、长久的喜悦和幸福。

## 5. NOCTURNE

Silence of the night a sad nocturnal①

Silence—Why does my soul tremble so?

I hear the humming② of my blood

And a soft storm passes through my brain.

Insomnia③! Not to be able to sleep and yet

To dream. I am the auto specimen

Of spiritual dissection the auto-Hamlet!

To dilute④ my sadness

In the wine of the night

In the marvelous crystal of the dark

And I ask myself: When will the dawn come?

Someone has closed a door

Someone has walked past—

The clock has rung three—If only it were

---

① nocturnal: adj. 夜的。
② hum: v. 发低哼声, 闭口哼歌, 嗡嗡叫; n. 嗡嗡声, 哼声, 杂声。
③ insomnia: n. 失眠（症）。
④ dilute: v. 冲淡, 稀释。

she！

—— Rubén Darío

### 夜　曲

夜晚的静寂，一首忧伤的夜曲的

静寂—— 谁让我的灵魂如此战栗？

我听到我的血液在嗡鸣，

一团温柔的风暴正穿过我的大脑。

失眠！已经无法入睡然而可以

做梦。我是精神被自动解剖了

的哈姆雷特样本。

稀释我的悲伤，

在夜晚的美酒中

在那黑暗的神秘水晶中——

我问我自己：那黎明何时来临？

有人关上了一扇门——

有人在散步经过——

时钟响了三下——这心难道只有她！——

作者：鲁文·达里奥（尼加拉瓜 1867~1916）

背景：鲁文·达里奥是拉丁美洲现代主义诗歌最重要的代表人物。达里奥的作品形式新颖，

致力于描写雅致的艺术珍品和异国的风貌,突出幻想的意境和悲观的情调等。他追求"纯粹的美",认为天鹅是美的象征,因在作品中反复描写这一意象而被称为"天鹅诗人"。他的诗韵律和谐,曾尝试使用九音节和十二音节的格律,研究改进六音步,最后采用了现代的自由诗体。鲁文·达里奥是个矛盾的诗人,这些矛盾是拉丁美洲民族文学曲折发展道路的反映。

6. I am forever walking upon these shores,
Betwixt the sand and the foam.
The high tide will erase my foot-prints,
And the wind will blow away the foam.
But the sea and the shore will remain
Forever.

—— Kahlil Gibran

我永远在这岸上行走,
在沙与沫之间。
高涨的潮水抹去我的足迹,
风也会把泡沫吹散。
但是大海和沙岸却会永存。

作者：纪·哈·纪伯伦（黎巴嫩 1883~1931）

出处：选自纪伯伦的名作《沙与沫》。

7. What language is thine①, O sea?
The language of eternal question.
What language is thy answer, O sky?
The language of eternal silence.
—— Rabindranath Tagore

海水呀，你说的是什么？
是永恒的疑问。
天空呀，你回答的是什么？
是永恒的沉默。

作者：泰戈尔（印度 1861~1941）
出处：选自泰戈尔的《飞鸟集》。

---

① thine：pron.
[古语、诗歌用语][thou 的所有格，作表语形容词，用于名词之后或单独使用][thou 的所有格，作修饰形容词，置于以元音或元音字母开头的名词前] 你的。

8. Stray birds of summer come to my window to sing and fly away. And yellow leaves of autumn, which have no songs, flutter① and fall there with a sigh.

——Rabindranath Tagore

夏天的失途鸟,来到我的窗前唱歌,又飞去了。

秋天的黄叶,它们没有什么可唱,扇动一下翅膀,一声叹息,落在那里。

作者:泰戈尔(印度 1861~1941)

出处:选自《飞鸟集》。

## 9. THE FURTHEST DISTANCE IN THE WORLD

The furthest distance in the world is not between life and death

But when I stand in front of you,

---

① flutter vi. 飘动;鼓翼;烦扰。
Vt. 拍;使焦急;使飘动。

Yet you don't know that I love you.

The furthest distance in the world is not when I stand in font of you,

Yet you can't see my love.

But when undoubtedly knowing the love from both,

Yet cannot be together.

The furthest distance in the world is not being apart while being in love.

But when plainly can not resist the yearning[①],

Yet pretending you have never been in my heart.

The furthest distance in the world is not when plainly can not resist the yearning,

Yet pretending you have never been in my heart.

But using one's indifferent heart,

To dig an uncrossable river for the one who loves you.

—— Rabindranath Tagore

---

① yearning n. 渴望；怀念；同情。

## 世界上最远的距离

世界上最遥远的距离,不是生与死,

而是我就站在你的面前,你却不知道我爱你。

世界上最遥远的距离,不是我站在你面前,你却不知道我爱你,

而是明明知道彼此相爱,却不能在一起。

世界上最遥远的距离,不是明明知道彼此相爱,却不能在一起,

而是明明无法抵挡这股思念,却还得故意装作丝毫没有把你放在心里。

世界上最遥远的距离,不是明明无法抵挡这股思念,

却还得故意装作丝毫没有把你放在心里,

而是用自己冷漠的心对爱你的人掘了一条无法跨越的沟渠。

作者:泰戈尔(印度 1861~1941)

出处:本诗选自《飞鸟集》(存争议)

10. I celebrate myself, and sing myself,

And what I assume① you shall assume,

For every atom belonging to me as good belongs to you.

I loaf and invite my soul,

I lean and loaf at my ease observing a spear of summer grass.

My tongue, every atom of my blood, formed from this soil, this air,

Born here of parents born here from parents the same, and their parents the same,

I, now thirty-seven years old in perfect health begin,

Hoping to cease not till death.

Creeds and schools in abeyance②,

Retiring back a while sufficed③ at what they are, but never forgotten,

I harbor for good or bad, I permit to

---

① assume: v. 假定，设想，承担。
② in abeyance: 悬而未决，犹未定夺。
③ sufficed: adj. 满足的。

speak at every hazard①,

Nature without check with original energy.

—— Walt Whitman

我赞美我自己,歌唱我自己,

我所讲的一切,将对你们也一样适合,

因为属于我的每一个原子,也同样属于你。

我邀请了我的灵魂一道闲游,

我俯身悠闲地观察一片夏日的草叶。

我的舌,我的血液的每个原子,是从这泥土这空气中形成,

我生在这里,我的父母生在这里,他们的父母也生在这里。

我,现在三十七岁,身体一开始就完全健康,

希望健康常驻,直到死亡。

教条和学派暂时搁在一边,

先隐退一会儿,满足于它们的现状,

---

① hazard:n. 冒险,危险,危害。

但绝不把它们遗忘，

　　不论是善是恶，我允许尽情地，毫不顾及地

　　用发自内心的活力讲述这大自然。

作者：沃尔特·惠特曼（美 1819~1892）

背景：选自惠特曼的《自我之歌》。惠特曼是美国 19 世纪最出名的浪漫主义诗人。阅读《自我之歌》，需要弄清两个问题。第一，"我"是谁？在这首诗中，"我"既是诗人又大于诗人，是具有美国民族特征和民主理想的巨人形象，也是新大陆的开拓者的形象。第二，主题是什么？笼统地讲，《自我之歌》反映了作者对人生哲学和宗教的观点。惠特曼将自我与美国、民主、宇宙意识等同，可见"个人主义"（individualism）在他心中已扎根颇深。美国特有的"个人主义"文化也发源于此。

惠特曼的《自我之歌》不仅在风格上开创了"自由体诗"的先河，而且将人类的思想觉悟提升到另一个高度，是世界文坛之瑰宝。

## 11. RED RIVER VALLEY

From this valley

They say you are going,
I shall miss your sweet face
And your smile,
For they say
You are taking the sunshine
That brightens our pathway a while.
Come and sit by my side if you love me,
Do not hasten to bid me adieu①,
But remember the Red River Valley,
And the girl that has loved you so true.
Won't you think of the valley you're leaving?
Oh how lonely, how sad it will be,
O think of the fond heart you're breaking
And the grief you are causing.
I have promised you, darling,
That never will a word from my lips cause you pain;
And my life, it will be yours forever
If you only will love me again.

---

① Adieu: n. 告别；辞行。

## 红河谷

人们说你就要离开村庄,

我们将怀念你的脸庞和微笑,

你的眼睛比太阳更明亮,

照耀在我们的心上。

走过来坐在我的身旁,

不要离别得这样匆忙,

要记住红河谷你的故乡,

还有那热爱你的姑娘。

你可会想到你的故乡,

多么寂寞多么凄凉,

想一想你走后我的痛苦,

想一想留给我的悲伤。

亲爱的人我曾经答应你,

我决不让你烦恼,

只要你能够重新爱我,

我愿意永远留在你身旁。

作者：不详

出处：加拿大北方民歌，上世纪 70 年代末 80 年代初这首《红河谷》在中国可谓家喻户晓。

12. Stand up, all victims of oppression,

For the tyrants[①] fear your might!

Don't cling so hard to your possessions.

For you have nothing, if you have no rights.

Let racist ignorance[②] be ended.

For respect makes the empires fall!

Freedom is merely privilege[③] extended.

Unless enjoyed by one and all.

So come brothers and sisters.

For the struggle carries on.

The Internationale,

Unites the world in song!

So comrades come rally[④].

For this is the time and place.

The international ideal

Unites the human race.

——Eugène Edine Pottier

---

① tyrant: n. 暴君。
② ignorance: n. 无知, 愚昧; 不知, 不懂。
③ privilege: n. 特权; 优待; 基本权利。
④ rally: vt. 集合; 团结。

起来，饥寒交迫的奴隶，
起来，全世界受苦的人！
满腔的热血已经沸腾，
要为真理而斗争！
旧世界打个落花流水，
奴隶们起来，起来！
不要说我们一无所有，
我们要做天下的主人！
这是最后的斗争，
团结起来，到明天，
英特那雄纳尔就一定要实现。
从来就没有什么救世主，
也不靠神仙皇帝，
要创造人类的幸福，
全靠我们自己。
我们要夺回劳动果实，
让思想冲破牢笼，
快把那炉火烧得通红，
趁热打铁才能成功！
最可恨那些毒蛇猛兽，
吃尽了我们的血肉，
一旦把它们消灭干净，
鲜红的太阳照遍全球。

作者：欧仁·鲍狄埃（法 1816~1887）

背景：《国际歌》歌词。1871 年 5 月 28 日，法国凡尔赛反动军队攻陷了世界上第一个无产阶级政权——巴黎公社的最后一个堡垒——贝尔·拉雪兹神甫公墓，标志革命失败。反动政府对全城革命者实施了大屠杀，无数革命志士倒在血泊中。面对着这一片白色恐怖，5 月 29 日，法国工人诗人鲍狄埃怀着满腔热血，奋笔疾书，写下了这曲气壮山河的歌词。这首诗歌原名为《国际工人联盟》，刊登在 1887 年出版的鲍狄埃的诗集《革命歌集》中。

## 13. BELLA CIAO

I woke this morning and all seemed peaceful

Bella ciao, bella ciao, bella ciao ciao ciao

I woke this morning and all seemed peaceful

But oppression[①] still exists.

Oh freedom fighter, I want to fight too

---

① oppression：n. 压迫；压制。

Bella ciao, bella ciao, bella ciao ciao ciao

Oh freedom fighter, I want to fight too

Against their living death.

And if I die, a freedom fighter,

Bella ciao, bella ciao, bella ciao ciao ciao

And if I die, a freedom fighter,

Then you'll have to bury me.

Let my body rest in the mountains

Bella ciao, bella ciao, bella ciao ciao ciao

Let my body rest in the mountains

In the shadow of my flower.

And all the people who will pass by there

Bella ciao, bella ciao, bella ciao ciao ciao

And all the people who will pass by there

Will show that lovely flower.

This is the blossom of those that died here

Bella ciao, bella ciao, bella ciao ciao ciao

This is the blossom of those that died here

For land and liberty.

## 再见朋友

那一天早晨,从梦中醒来

啊朋友再见吧再见吧再见吧

一天早晨从梦中醒来

侵略者闯进我的家

啊游击队啊快带我走吧

啊朋友再见吧再见吧再见吧

游击队啊快带我走吧

我实在不能再忍受

啊如果我在战斗中牺牲

啊朋友再见吧再见吧再见吧

如果我在战斗中牺牲

你一定把我来埋葬

请把我埋在高高的山岗

啊朋友再见吧再见吧再见吧

把我埋在高高的山岗

再插上一朵美丽的花

啊每当人们从这里走过

啊朋友再见吧再见吧再见吧

每当人们从这里走过

都说啊多么美丽的花

那一天早晨从梦中醒来

啊朋友再见吧再见吧再见吧

一天早晨从梦中醒来

我即将离开我家乡

出处：意大利民歌

背景：《啊！朋友再见！》是意大利民歌，后在意大利游击队中流传，表达了二战中法西斯占领和统治下的人民不畏强暴勇于反抗并且乐观面对困难的精神。这首歌被前南斯拉夫影片《桥》用作主题曲，因此被很多人误认为是南斯拉夫民歌。

# 外国散文小说节选

1. It is for us the living, rather, to be dedicated[①] here to the unfinished work which they who fought here have thus far so nobly advanced. It is rather for us to be here dedicated to the great task remaining before us: that from these honored dead we take increased devotion to that cause for which they gave the last full measure of devotion; that we here highly resolve that these dead shall not have died in vain; that this nation, under God, shall have a new birth of freedom; and that government of the people, by the people, for the people,[②] shall not perish[③] from the earth.

—— Abraham Lincoln

## 我们活着的人应该在这块土地上献

---

① dedicated: adj. 专注的，献身的。

② government of the people, by the people, for the people: 民有、民治、民享的政府。

③ not perish: 永存；这里采用的是"反说正译"的翻译方法。

身于那些曾在此处奋斗所努力推展却尚未完成的工作。我们实在应该献身于这些勇者所遗留给我们的眼前这个伟大的任务：这些光荣过世的先烈们曾为国家大业奉献到底，而我们则应秉承他们的奉献精神，更加全力以赴；我们决意不让这些先烈白白牺牲；在上帝的庇护之下，自由将在我国重生，而这个民有、民治、民享的政府将永存于世上。

作者：亚伯拉罕·林肯（美 1809~1865）

背景：这是美国第16任总统林肯于1863年11月19日在葛底斯堡国家烈士公墓落成典礼上发表的一篇激动人心、誉满全球、简短精炼的演说。葛底斯堡演说缅怀为国家稳定团结而牺牲的烈士，激励人民继承烈士精神，继续为国家建设而奋斗。

2. To go into solitude①, a man needs to retire as much from his chamber② as from

---

① solitude：n. 孤独；独居；荒僻之地，幽静的地方。

② chamber：n. 房间，（尤指）卧室，寝室。

society. I am not solitary① whilst I read and write, though nobody is with me. But if a man would be alone, let him look at the stars. The rays that come from those heavenly② worlds will separate between him and vulgar③ things. One might think the atmosphere was made transparent with this design, to give man, in the heavenly bodies, the perpetual presence of the sublime④. Seem in the streets of cities, how great they are! If the stars should appear one night in a thousand years, how would men believe and adore; and preserve for many generations the remembrance⑤ of the city of God which had been shown! But every night come out these preachers of beauty, and

---

① solitary: adj. 孤独的，唯一的。
② heavenly: adj. 天上的，神圣的，天国似的。
③ vulgar: adj. 粗俗的。
④ sublime: adj. 壮观的，卓越的。
⑤ remembrance: n. 回想，记忆，纪念品。

light the universe with their admonishing① smile.

—— Ralph Waldo Emerson

走入孤独,远离书斋,如同远离社会一样重要。纵然无人在我身旁,当我读书或写作时,并非独处一隅。如果一个人渴望独处,就请他注目于星辰吧。那从天界传来的光芒,使人们得以脱离可触摸的现世。可以这样说,我们假想,大气之所以透明,就是为了让人们总能看到天国的灿烂光芒。从普通城市的街道向上看,它们是如此深邃伟岸。假如星辰千年一现,人类关于上帝之城的记忆,必将世代相传,为人们长久地信仰着,珍存着,崇拜着。然而,每一晚,这些美的使者都会降临,以它们劝诫人间的微笑,照亮宇宙。

作者:拉尔夫·沃尔多·爱默生(美 1803~1882)
出处:《论自然》

---

① admonish:v. 劝告,训诫,告诫。

背景：爱默生是美国思想家、诗人。《论自然》是他的代表作，也是"超验主义"的最好体现。爱默生在《论自然》中提出：人应该独立寻求与上帝交流；人的灵魂（有限精神）分享有上帝神性（无限精神）的思想；自然作为上帝精神的物化体现，是人与上帝交流的唯一途径。他的这种整体主义的自然观，启迪了一种新的整体主义的思维方式：把自然的本质归结于生命共同体，从自然共同体的高度在人与自然之间建立一种平等、和谐的关系。

## 3. GARMENTS

Upon a day Beauty and Ugliness met on the shore of a sea. And they said to one another, "Let us bathe in the sea."

Then they disrobed[①] and swam in the waters.

And after a while Ugliness came back to shore and garmented himself with the garments of Beauty and walked away.

And Beauty too came out of the sea, and

---

① disrobe：v. 使脱光；脱去……的衣服。

found not her raiment, and she was too shy to be naked, therefore she dressed herself with the raiment of Ugliness. And Beauty walked her way.

And to this very day men and women mistake the one for the other.

Yet some there are who have beheld the face of Beauty, and they know her notwithstanding her garments. And some there are who know the face of Ugliness, and the cloth conceals him not from their eyes.

—— Kahlil Gibran

## 外 衣

一天,美和丑在海岸上相遇了,于是相约去海里沐浴。

来到海边,脱下外衣,她们便畅游起来。过了一会儿,丑回到岸边,换上美的衣服溜走了。

美从水里出来,发现自己的衣服不见了,又不好意思光着身子,只好穿上丑的衣服,离开了。

于是直到今天，男人和女人仍将美丑认错。

然而，也有那么些人，他们目睹过美的芳容，因此总能认出美，不管她身着何衣。

而另一些人见过丑的真面，对他们来说，丑还是丑，哪怕有华袍裹身。

作者：纪·哈·纪伯伦（黎巴嫩（1883－1931）

出处：《流浪者》

## 4. ON CHILDREN

And a woman who held a babe against her bosom said, "Speak to us of Children."

And he said:

Your children are not your children.

They are the sons and daughters of Life's longing for itself.

They come through you but not from you,

And though they are with you, yet they belong not to you.

You may give them your love but not your thoughts.

For they have their own thoughts.

You may house their bodies but not their souls,

For their souls dwell in the house of tomorrow, which you cannot visit, not even in your dreams.

You may strive to be like them, but seek not to make them like you.

For life goes not backward nor tarries with yesterday.

You are the bows from which your children as living arrows are sent forth.

The archer sees the mark upon the path of the infinite, and He bends you with His might that His arrows may go swift and far.

Let your bending in the archer's hand be for gladness;

For even as he loves the arrow that flies, so he loves also the bow that is stable.

—— Kahlil Gibran

## 论孩子

于是一个怀中抱着孩子的妇人说,先知请给我们谈孩子。

他说:

你们的孩子,都不是你们的孩子。

乃是生命自身憧憬的儿女。

他们是凭借你们而来,却不是因你们而来,

他们虽和你们同在,却不属于你们。

你们可以给他们以爱,却不可给他们以思想。

因为他们有自己的思想。

你们也许可以庇护他们的身体,却不可能荫庇他们的灵魂。

因为他们的灵魂,栖息于明日,那是你们即使在梦中也不能到达的。

你们可以努力去变得和他们一样,却不可以让他们变得和你们一样。

因为生命是不倒行的,也不与昨日一同停留。

你们是弓,你们的孩子是从弦上发出的生命的箭矢。

那射者在无尽的前路上中看定了目

标，也用神力将你们引满，使他的箭矢射得迅速而遥远。

让你们在射者手中的弯曲中怀着愉快的心情吧；

因为他爱那飞出的箭，也就爱了那稳定的弓。

作者：纪·哈·纪伯伦（黎巴嫩 1883~1931）

背景：《论孩子》出自纪伯伦的散文集《先知》。《先知》是纪伯伦的代表作，以一位智者临别赠言的方式，论述爱与美、生与死、婚姻与家庭、劳作与安乐、法律与自由、理智与热情、善恶与宗教等一系列人生和社会问题，充满东方色彩的比喻和哲理。

5. Do you think, because I am poor, obscure[①], plain, and little, I am soulless and heartless? You think wrong! —I have as much soul as you—and full as much heart! And if God had

---

① obscure：adj. 模糊的；晦涩的；昏暗的。

gifted me with some beauty and much wealth, I should have made it as hard for you to leave me, as it is now for me to leave you. I am not talking to you now through the medium of custom, conventionalities①, nor even of mortal flesh: it is my spirit that addresses your spirit; just as if both had passed through the grave②, and we stood at God's feet, equal—as we are!

—— Charlotte Bronte

你以为我穷，低微，不漂亮，个子小，我就没有灵魂没有心吗？你想错了！我和你一样有灵魂，有一颗完整的心！要是上帝赐予我一点姿色和充足的财富，我会使你难以离开我就如同我现在难以离开你一样，我现在不是依据习俗、常规，甚至也不是通过血肉之躯同你说话，而是我的灵魂同你的灵魂在对话，就仿

---

① conventionalities：n. 惯例；习俗；老套。
② grave：n. 墓穴，坟墓。

佛我们两人穿过坟墓，站在上帝脚下，彼此平等——本来就如此！"

作者：夏洛蒂·勃朗特（英 1816~1855）

出处：小说《简·爱》

背景：《简·爱》是一部带有自传色彩的长篇小说，它阐释了这样一个主题：人的价值＝尊严＋爱。《简·爱》中的女主人公简爱人生追求有两个基本旋律：富有激情、幻想和反抗、坚持不懈的精神；对人间自由幸福的渴望和对更高精神境界的追求。这部小说通过叙述孤女坎坷不平的人生经历，成功地塑造了一个不安于现状、不甘受辱、敢于抗争的女性形象，反映一个平凡心灵的坦诚倾诉、呼号和责难以及由一个小写的人成为一个大写的人的渴望。

6. They said of him that it was the most peaceful face ever seen there. What passed through Sydney Carton's mind as he walked those last steps to his death? Perhaps he saw into the future...

'I see Barsad, Defarge, the judges, all dying under this terrible machine. I see a beautiful city being built in this terrible place. I see that new people will live here, in real freedom. I see the lives for whom I give my life, happy and peaceful in that England which I shall never see again. I see Lucie when she is old, crying for me on this day every year, and I know that she and her husband remember me until their deaths. I see their son, who has my name, now a man. I see him become a famous lawyer and make my name famous by his work. I hear him tell his son my story.

It is a far, far better thing that I do, than I have ever done; it is a far far better rest than I go to, than I have ever known.'

—— Charles John Huffam Dickens

人们谈论他说他的脸是在那种地方见过的最平静的脸。当西德尼·卡登迈着最后的步伐向死亡走去时,他的脑海中想到了什么呢?也许他看到了未来……

"我看到巴萨德、德法热、法官们都在这个可怕的机器下面死去。我看见一

个美丽的城市正在这片可怕的土地上建立起来。我看到新一代的人民将在真正的自由中生活。我看到我为之付出生命的人们,他们幸福安宁地生活在我再也见不到的英国。我看见路西年老的时候,每一年的这一天都会为我哭泣,我知道她和她的丈夫会一直到死都记着我。我看见他们的儿子,有着和我一样的名字,现在长成了一个男人。我看见他成了一位著名的律师并通过他的工作而使我扬名四方。我听见他给他的儿子讲起我的故事。

我做的是一件很好的事。它远远好过我所做的所有的事。它将是一个很好的归宿,远比我所知道的要好。"

作者:查尔斯·狄更斯(英 1812~1870)

出处:小说《双城记》

背景:《双城记》是描述法国大革命一部大时代长篇历史小说。"双城"指的是巴黎与伦敦。后来被改编拍摄成多个版本的电影,也有音乐专辑以此为名。

查尔斯·狄更斯,19世纪英国批判现实主义小说家。狄更斯特别注意描写生活在英国社会底层的"小人物"的生活遭遇，深刻地反映了当时英国复杂的社会现实，为英国批判现实主义文学的开拓和发展做出了卓越的贡献。他的作品至今依然盛行，对英国文学发展起到了深远的影响。主要作品有《匹克威克外传》、《雾都孤儿》、《老古玩店》、《艰难时世》、《我们共同的朋友》等。

7. The founders of a new colony, whatever Utopia① of human virtue and happiness they might originally project, have invariably recognised it among their earliest practical necessities to allot② a portion of the virgin soil as a cemetery③, and another portion as the site of a prison. In accordance with this rule, it may safely be assumed that the forefathers④ of Boston had built the first

---

① Utopia：n. 乌托邦（理想中最美好的社会）；理想国。
② allot：vt. 分配；拨给；分派。
③ cemetery：n. 墓地；公墓。
④ forefather：n. 祖先；前辈。

prison-house somewhere in the vicinity① of Cornhill, almost as seasonably as they marked out the first burial-ground, on Isaac Johnson's lot, and round about his grave, which subsequently became the nucleus② of all the congregated③ sepulchers④ in the old churchyard of King's Chapel⑤. Certain it is that, some fifteen or twenty years after the settlement of the town, the wooden jail was already marked with weather-stains and other indications of age, which gave a yet darker aspect to its beetle-browed⑥ and gloomy front. The rust on the ponderous⑦

---

① vicinity: n. 邻近,附近;近处。
② nucleus: n. 核,核心;原子核。
③ congregated: adj. 集合在一起的。
④ sepulcher: n. 坟墓。
⑤ chapel: n. 礼拜;小礼拜堂,小教堂。
⑥ beetle-browed: adj. 粗眉毛的,浓眉的;皱眉头的。
⑦ ponderous: adj. 笨重的;沉闷的;呆板的。

iron-work of its oaken door looked more antique① than anything else in the New World. Like all that pertains② to crime, it seemed never to have known a youthful era. Before this ugly edifice③, and between it and the wheel-track of the street, was a grass-plot, much overgrown with burdock④, pig-weed, apple-pern, and such unsightly vegetation, which evidently found something congenial⑤ in the soil that had so early borne the black flower of civilised society, a prison. But, on one side of the portal, and rooted almost at the threshold⑥, was a wild rose-bush, covered, in this month of June,

---

① antique: adj. 古老的，年代久远的；过时的。
② pertain: vi. 从属；属于；附属（经常与to连用）。
③ edifice: n. 大厦；大建筑物。
④ burdock: n. 牛蒡。
⑤ congenial: adj. 意气相投的；性格相似的；适意的；一致的。
⑥ threshold: n. 极限；门槛；入口。

with its delicate gems, which might be imagined to offer their fragrance and fragile beauty to the prisoner as he went in, and to the condemned criminal as he came forth to his doom, in token that the deep heart of Nature could pity and be kind to him.

—— Nathaniel Hawthorne

新殖民地的开拓者们，不管他们的头脑中起初有什么关于人类品德和幸福的美妙理想，总要在各种实际需要的草创之中，忘不了划出一片未开垦的处女地充当墓地，再择出另一片土地来修建监狱。根据这一惯例，我们可以有把握地推断：波士顿的先民们在谷山一带的某处地方修建第一座监狱，同在艾萨克·约翰逊地段标出头一块墓地几乎是在同一时期。后来便以他的坟墓为核心，扩展成国王教堂的那块成片的古老墓地。可以确定无疑地说，早在镇子建立十五年或二十年之际，那座木造监狱就已经因风吹日晒和岁月的流逝而为它那狰狞和阴森的门面增加了几分晦暗凄楚的景象，使它那橡木大门沉重铁艺上的斑斑锈痕比新大陆任何陈迹都益发古老。象一切与罪恶二字息息相关的事物一样，这座监狱似乎从来不曾经历过自己的青春韶华。从这座丑陋的大房子门前，一直到轧着车辙的街道，有一片草地，上面过于繁茂地簇生着牛蒡、茨藜、毒莠等等这类不堪入目的杂草，这些杂草显然在这块土地上找到了共通的东西，因为正是在这块土地上早早便诞生了文明社会的黑花——监狱。然而，在大门的一侧，几乎就在门槛处，有一丛野玫瑰挺然而立，在这六月时分，盛开着精致的宝石般的花朵，这会使人想象，它们是在向步入牢门的囚犯或跨出阴暗牢房的即将被处极刑的囚犯奉献着自己的芬芳和妩媚，借以表示在大自然深深的心扉中，仍存着对他们的一丝怜悯和仁慈。

作者：纳撒尼尔·霍桑（美 1804~1864）

出处：小说《红字》

背景：纳撒尼尔·霍桑是美国19世纪影响最

大的浪漫主义小说家、美国文学史上第一个写作短篇小说的作家，也是美国文学浪漫主义文学中的心理分析小说的开创者。爱伦·坡称他的小说"属于艺术的最高层次，一种服从于非常崇高级别的天才的艺术。"

他最重要的长篇小说《红字》，以殖民地时期新英格兰生活为背景，描写一个受不合理的婚姻束缚的少妇犯了为加尔文教派所严禁的通奸罪而被示众，暴露了当时政教合一体制统治下殖民地社会中的某些黑暗。作者细致地描写了经过长期赎罪而在精神上自新的少妇海斯特·白兰，长期受到信仰和良心的责备而终于坦白承认了罪过的狄姆斯台尔牧师以及满怀复仇心理以至完全丧失人性的白兰的丈夫罗杰，层层深入地探究了有关罪恶和人性的各种道德、哲理问题。小说以监狱和玫瑰花开场，以墓地结束，充满丰富的象征意义。

# 外国影视戏剧作品节选

1. To be, or not to be—that is the question:
Whether 'tis nobler in the mind to suffer
The slings① and arrows of outrageous② fortune,
Or to take arms against a sea of troubles,
And by opposing end them?

—— William Shakespeare

生存还是毁灭,这是一个值得考虑的问题;

默然忍受命运的暴虐的毒箭,

或是挺身反抗人世的无涯的苦难,

通过斗争把它们扫清,

这两种行为,

哪一种更高贵?

作者:莎士比亚(英 1564~1616)

出处:《哈姆雷特》第三幕,第一场

背景:威廉·莎士比亚是英国文艺复兴时期

---

① sling: n. 投石器,抛掷,吊物机; slings and arrows 译为"毒箭"。

② outrageous: adj. 暴虐的,极无礼的,可恶的,惊人的,肆无忌惮的,毫无节制的。

最著名的、也是享誉世界的剧作家和诗人。文艺复兴时期的代表文化是人文主义（humanism），而莎士比亚的作品之所以成为经典，也在于他们谈论着人类永恒的话题：人性。上文哈姆雷特的自白就充分表现了他在面对是否刺杀篡位杀父的叔父时犹豫、痛苦的心情。

2. Enter MUSICIANS

LORENZO. Come, ho, and wake Diana with a hymn;

With sweetest touches pierce your mistress' ear.

And draw her home with music.
[Music]

JESSICA. I am never merry when I hear sweet music.

LORENZO. The reason is your spirits are attentive;

For do but note a wild and wanton herd,

Or race of youthful and unhandled colts,

Fetching mad bounds, bellowing and neighing loud,

Which is the hot condition of their blood;If

they but hear perchance a trumpet sound,

Or any air of music touch their ears,

You shall perceive them make a mutual stand,

Their savage eyes turn'd to a modest gaze

By the sweet power of music. Therefore the poet

Did feign that Orpheus drew trees, stones, and floods;

Since nought so stockish, hard, and full of rage,

But music for the time doth change his nature.

The man that hath no music in himself,

Nor is not mov'd with concord of sweet sounds,

Is fit for treasons, stratagems, and spoils;

The motions of his spirit are dull: as night,

And his affections dark as Erebus.

Let no such man be trusted. Mark the music.

——William Shakespeare

众乐工上。

罗兰佐：来啊！奏起一支圣歌来唤醒狄安娜女神；用最温柔的节奏倾注到你们女主人的耳中，让她被乐声吸引着回来。(音乐。)

杰西卡：我听见了柔和的音乐，总觉得有些惆怅。

罗兰佐：这是因为你有一个敏感的灵魂。你只要看一群不服管束的畜生，或是那野性未驯的小马，逗着它们奔放的血气，乱跳狂奔，高声嘶叫，倘然偶尔听到一声喇叭，或是任何乐调，就会一齐立定，它们狂野的眼光，因为中了音乐的魅力，变成温和的注视。所以诗人会造出俄耳甫斯用音乐感动木石、平息风浪的故事，因为无论怎样坚硬顽固狂暴的事物，音乐都可以立刻改变它们的性质；灵魂里没有音乐，或是听了甜蜜和谐的乐声而不会感动的人，都是擅于为非作恶、使奸弄诈的；他们的灵魂像黑夜一样昏沉，他们的感情像鬼域一样幽暗；这种人是不可信任的。听这音乐！

作者：莎士比亚（英 1564～1616）

出处：《威尼斯商人》

背景：《威尼斯商人》是莎士比亚早期创作的一部喜剧。这时期英国正当伊丽莎白女王统治的盛世，英国成了统一的民族国家。新兴资产阶级刚登上历史舞台，人文主义者生气蓬勃。他们提倡人权自由．个性解放，反对封建割据和教会的统治。这就使莎士比亚的喜剧充满了乐观主义的色彩。《威尼斯商人》就表现了新兴的商业资本对封建的高利贷资本的胜利，歌颂了人文主义的友谊、爱情及个性的自由解放。

3. What though the field be lost?
   All is not lost; the unconquerable Will,
   And study of revenge, immortal hate,
   And courage never to submit or yield:
   And what is else not to be overcome?

That Glory never shall his wrath[①] or might

Extort[②] from me. To bow and sue for grace

With suppliant[③] knee, and deifie his power,

Who from the terrour of this Arm so late

Doubted his Empire, that were low indeed,

That were an ignominy[④] and shame beneath

This downfall

——John Milton

我们损失了什么？

并非什么都丢光：不挠的意志、

热切的复仇心、不灭的憎恨，

以及永不屈服，永不退让的勇气，

还有什么比这些更难战胜的呢？

---

① Wrath: n. 愤怒，狂怒
② Extort: v. 勒索，逼取
③ Suppliant: adj. 恳求的，哀求的，谦卑的
④ ignominy: n. 耻辱，污辱

他的暴怒也罢,威力也罢,
决不能夺去我这份光荣。
经过这一场战争的惨烈,
好容易使他的政权动摇;
这时我们还要弯腰曲膝,向他
哀求怜悯,拜倒在他的权力之下,
那才真正是卑鄙、可耻,
比这次的沉沦还要卑贱。

作者:约翰·弥尔顿(英 1608~1674)

出处:《失乐园》

背景:英国诗人、政论家,民主斗士。弥尔顿是清教徒文学的代表,他的一生都在为资产阶级民主运动而奋斗,代表作《失乐园》是和《荷马史诗》、《神曲》并称为西方三大诗歌。《失乐园》以史诗一般的磅礴气势揭示了人的原罪与堕落,体现了诗人追求自由的崇高精神,是世界文学史、思想史上的一部极重要的作品。

4. Alas! The generations of men

   in their effort, honor, achievement, their pride…

   and in the end it comes to nothing.

What man, after chasing all his life

for the shadow of happiness, can claim

more than a moment's illusion?

Oedipus, your fate

is a chilling example.

You had everything that makes for happiness,

and in a moment, it's gone.

——Sophocles

凡人的子孙啊，我把你们的生命当作一场空！谁的幸福不是表面现象，一会儿就消灭了？不幸的俄狄浦斯，你的命运，你的命运警告我不要说凡人是幸福的。

作者：索福克勒斯（古希腊公元前496～公元前406）

出处：《俄狄浦斯王》

背景：索福克勒斯（雅典人，雅典三大悲剧作家之一，年轻时就表现出了杰出的音乐才能。索福克勒斯一生创作了120多部剧本，但现在完整保留下来的悲剧只有《埃阿斯》《安提戈涅》

《俄狄浦斯王》《埃勒克特拉》《特拉基斯少女》《菲罗克忒忒斯》《俄狄浦斯在科洛诺斯》等七部。《俄狄浦斯王》：是索福克勒斯的代表作，以希腊神话中关于忒拜王室的故事为题材，紧紧围绕俄狄浦斯杀父娶母的预言和寻找凶手这两条线索展开。这是一部十分悲惨的剧作，主要表现的是个人意志与命运的冲突，英雄人物在面对厄运中显示了人的精神的神圣崇高。剧作结构复杂而严谨，亚里士多德认为该剧是希腊悲剧的典范。

5. What is life but a series of inspired follies[①]? The difficulty is to find them to do. Never lose a chance: it doesn't come every day. I shall make a duchess[②] of this draggletailed[③] guttersnipe[④].

——George Bernard Shaw

　　人生是什么，还不是趁着一时困难高兴而做一系列的糊涂事？困难只是没

---

① folly：n. 愚蠢，荒唐事
② duchess：n. 公爵夫人，女公爵
③ draggletailed：adj. 拖着长裙子的，堕落的
④ guttersnipe：n. 贫民窟的小孩儿，流浪儿

有机会去做。不要放过一个机会，机会不是每天都有的。我一定要把这个破烂的叫化子变成公爵夫人。

作者：乔治·伯纳德·萧伯纳（爱尔兰 1856~1950）

出处：《卖花女》

背景：萧伯纳，现代杰出的现实主义戏剧作家，是世界著名的擅长幽默与讽刺的语言大师。萧伯纳的戏剧最突出的特点是紧密结合现实政治斗争，敢于触及资本主义社会最本质的问题，把剥削阶级的丑恶嘴脸暴露在公众面前。

6. ANYA. [Laughs] Thanks to the tramp who frightened Barbara, we're alone now.

TROFIMOV. Varya's afraid we may fall in love with each other and won't get away from us for days on end. Her narrow mind won't allow her to understand that we are above love. To escape all the petty and deceptive[①] things which prevent our being

---

① deceptive：adj. 欺骗的

happy and free, that is the aim and meaning of our lives. Forward! We go irresistibly[①] on to that bright star which burns there, in the distance! Don't lag behind, friends!

ANYA. [Clapping her hands] How beautifully you talk! [Pause] It is glorious here today!

TROFIMOV. Yes, the weather is wonderful.

ANYA. What have you done to me, Peter? I don't love the cherry orchard[②] as I used to. I loved it so tenderly, I thought there was no better place in the world than our orchard.

TROFIMOV. All Russia is our orchard. The land is great and beautiful, there are many marvellous places in it. [Pause] Think, Anya, your grandfather, your great-grandfather, and all your ancestors were serf-owners, they owned living souls; and

---

① irresistibly: adv. 难以抗拒地
② orchard: n. 果园

now, doesn't something human look at you from every cherry in the orchard, every leaf and every stalk? Don't you hear voices...? Oh, it's awful, your orchard is terrible; and when in the evening or at night you walk through the orchard, then the old bark on the trees sheds a dim light and the old cherry-trees seem to be dreaming of all that was a hundred, two hundred years ago, and are oppressed by their heavy visions. Still, at any rate, we've left those two hundred years behind us. So far we've gained nothing at all——we don't yet know what the past is to be to us——we only philosophize[①], we complain that we are dull, or we drink vodka. For it's so clear that in order to begin to live in the present we must first redeem the past, and that can only be done by suffering, by strenuous, uninterrupted labour. Understand that, Anya.

ANYA. The house in which we live has

---

① philosophize: v. 推究哲理,进行哲学探讨

long ceased to be our house; I shall go away. I give you my word.

TROFIMOV. If you have the housekeeping keys, throw them down the well and go away. Be as free as the wind.

ANYA. [Enthusiastically] How nicely you said that!

TROFIMOV. Believe me, Anya, believe me! I'm not thirty yet, I'm young, I'm still a student, but I have undergone a great deal! I'm as hungry as the winter, I'm ill, I'm shaken. I'm as poor as a beggar, and where haven't I been——fate has tossed me everywhere! But my soul is always my own; every minute of the day and the night it is filled with unspeakable presentiments[①]. I know that happiness is coming, Anya, I see it already...

ANYA. [Thoughtful] The moon is rising.

——Anton chekhov

---

① presentiment: n. 预感

安尼雅：（笑）多谢那个过路人，把瓦丽雅吓跑了，现在就剩我们两个人。

特罗菲莫夫：瓦丽雅怕我们突然相爱，就整天盯着我们。她那偏狭的脑袋无法理解，我们是爱情至上者。我们的生活的目标和意义，是在于要摆脱一切渺小的、虚幻的东西，它们妨碍我们成为一个自由而幸福的人。前进！我们要奋不顾身地走向那颗闪闪发光的星星，它闪耀在遥远的天际！前进！朋友们，不要停止你的步伐！

安尼雅：（挥舞着手臂）你说得多好！（停顿）今天这里太美了！

特罗菲莫夫：是的，多好的天气。

安尼雅：彼嘉，你给我的影响好大呀，我为什么不像从前那样地爱樱桃园了呢。我以前是那样地爱着它，心想世上再没有比我们的花园更美的地方了。

特罗菲莫夫：整个俄罗斯都是我们的花园。世界大得很，美得很，美丽的地方有的是。（停顿）安尼雅，您倒是想想您的祖父、曾祖父和您所有的祖先，都是占有活的灵魂的农奴主,人的精灵难道不是从花园里的每一棵樱桃树上,从每一片树叶上,从每一个树干上向您张望,您难道没有听到他们的声音……占有活得灵魂——这件事把所有的你们——过去活着的和现在活着的人都给腐蚀了,您的母亲,您,您的舅舅没有意识到你们欠着别人的债,你们是靠着别人,靠着那些你们不容许走进自家内院的穷人过活的。噢,这很可怕,你们的樱桃园很可怕,当黄昏时分或者深夜里走过花园,那樱桃树的粗老的树皮发出幽暗的光,好像樱桃树在梦中看到了一二百年前的情景,沉睡的恶梦压抑着她们。是的,我们落后了,落后了至少两百年,我们一事无成,对历史的过去没有明确的态度,我们只知道空发议论,只知道埋怨乏味的生活,要不就是狂饮伏特加酒。要知道这是很清楚的,如果想要生活在今天,就需要补偿过去,和它来个了结,而要补偿过去,就需要感受痛苦,就需要不知疲倦地劳作。安尼雅,您要知道这一点。

安尼雅：我们居住的这所房子早就不属于我们了，我要离开这里，我向您保证。

特罗菲莫夫：如果您手里有家里的钥匙，就把它们扔进井里去，然后离家出走。您要做自由的人，像风一样自由。

安尼雅：（兴奋异常）您说得多美！

特罗菲莫夫：安尼雅，请您相信我！我还不到三十岁，我年轻，我还是个大学生，但我已经经历过很多磨难！一到冷天，饥饿和疾病就向我袭来，我就苦恼万分，穷得像个乞丐。命运驱使我不停奔波，浪迹天涯！但尽管这样，无论是白天还是黑夜，我的心里永远充满着无法言喻的预感。我预感到幸福的临近，安尼雅，我已经能看到它……

安尼雅：（沉思地）月亮升起来了。

作者：安东·契诃夫（俄 1860~1904）

出处：《樱桃园》

背景：俄国小说家、戏剧家、十九世纪末期俄国批判现实主义作家、短篇小说艺术大师。他和法国的莫泊桑，美国的欧·亨利齐名为三大短篇小说巨匠。剧本《樱桃园》展示了贵族的无可避免的没落和由新兴资产阶级所代替的历史过程，同时表现了毅然同过去告别和向往幸福未来的乐观情绪：樱桃园伐木的斧声伴随着"新生活万岁！"的欢呼声。

7. Nora. What do you consider my most sacred duties?

Helmer. Do I need to tell you that? Are they not your duties to your husband and your children?

Nora. I have other duties just as sacred.

Helmer. That you have not. What duties could those be?

Nora. Duties to myself.

Helmer. Before all else, you are a wife and a mother.

Nora. I don't believe that any longer. I believe that before all else I am a reasonable human being, just as you are— or, at all events, that I must try and become one. I know quite well, Torvald, that most people would think you right, and that views of that kind are to be found in books; but I can no longer content myself with what most people say, or with what is found in books. I must think over things for myself and get to understand them.

Helmer. Can you not understand your place in your own home? Have you not a reliable guide in such matters as that? — have you no religion?

Nora. I am afraid, Torvald, I do not exactly know what religion is.

Helmer. What are you saying?

Nora. I know nothing but what the clergyman [①]said, when I went to be confirmed. He told us that religion was this, and that, and the other. When I am away from all this, and am alone, I will look into that matter too. I will see if what the clergyman said is true, or at all events if it is true for me.

---

① clergyman: n. 牧师,教士

Helmer. This is unheard of in a girl of your age! But if religion cannot lead you aright, let me try and awaken your conscience. I suppose you have some moral sense? Or— answer me— am I to think you have none?

Nora. I assure you, Torvald, that is not an easy question to answer. I really don't know. The thing perplexes① me altogether. I only know that you and I look at it in quite a different light. I am learning, too, that the law is quite another thing from what I supposed; but I find it impossible to convince myself that the law is right. According to it a woman has no right to spare her old dying father, or to save her husband's life. I can't believe that.

Helmer. You talk like a child. You don't understand the conditions of the world in which you live.

Nora. No, I don't. But now I am going to

---

① perplex: v. 使迷惑，使困惑

try. I am going to see if I can make out who is right, the world or I.

——Henrik Johan Ibsen

娜拉：你说什么是我最神圣的责任？

海尔茂：那还用我说？你最神圣的责任是你对丈夫和儿女的责任。

娜拉：我还有别的同样神圣的责任。

海尔茂：没有的事！你说的是什么责任？

娜拉：我说的是我对自己的责任。

海尔茂：别的不用说，首先你是一个老婆，一个母亲。

娜拉：这些话现在我都不信了。现在我只信，首先我是一个人，跟你一样的一个人——至少我要学做一个人；托伐，我知道大多数人赞成你的话，并且书本里也是这么说。可是从今以后我不能一味相信大多数人说的话，也不能一味相信书本里说的话。什么事情我都要用自己脑子想一想，把事情的道理弄明白。

海尔茂：难道你不明白你在自己家庭的地位？难道在这些问题上没有颠扑

不破的道理指导你？难道你不信仰宗教？

娜拉：托伐，不瞒你说，我真不知道宗教是什么。

海尔茂：你这话怎么讲？

娜拉：除了行坚信礼的时候牧师对我说的那套话，我什么都不知道。牧师告诉过我，宗教是这个，宗教是那个。等我离开这儿一个人过日子的时候我也要把宗教问题仔细想一想。我要仔细想一想牧师告诉我的话究竟对不对，对我合用不合用。

海尔茂：喔，从来没听说过这种话！并且还是从这么个年轻女人嘴里说出来的！要是宗教不能带你走正路，让我唤醒你的良心来帮助你——你大概还有点道德观念吧？要是没有，你就干脆说没有。

娜拉：托伐，这小问题不容易回答。我实在不明白。这些事情我摸不清。我只知道我的想法跟你的想法完全不一样。我也听说，国家的法律跟我心里想的不一样，可是我不信那些法律是正确的。父亲病得快死了，法律不许女儿给他省

烦恼，丈夫病得快死了，法律不许老婆想法子救他的性命！我不信世界上有这种不讲理的法律。

海尔茂：你说这些话像个小孩子。你不了解咱们的社会。

娜拉 我真不了解。现在我要去学习。我一定要弄清楚，究竟是社会正确，还是我正确。

作者：亨利克·约翰·易卜生（挪 1828～1906）

出处：《玩偶之家》

背景：易卜生是一位影响深远的挪威剧作家，被认为是现代现实主义戏剧的创始人。三幕话剧《玩偶之家》是易卜生的代表作，主要写主人公娜拉从爱护丈夫、信赖丈夫到与丈夫决裂，最后离家出走，摆脱玩偶地位的自我觉醒过程。《玩偶之家》曾被比做"妇女解放运动的宣言书"。在这个宣言书里，娜拉终于觉悟到自己在家庭中的玩偶地位，并向丈夫严正地宣称："首先我是一个人，跟你一样的人至少我要学做一个人。"以此作为对以男权为中心的社会传统观念的反叛。

8. Women of Corinth, I have stepped outside so you will not condemn me. Many people act superior—I'm well aware of this.

Some keep it private; some are arrogant in public view. Yet there are other people who, just because they lead a quiet life, are thought to be aloof. There is no justice in human eyesight: people take one look and hate a man, before they know his heart, though no injustice has been done to them. A foreigner must adapt to a new city, certainly. Nor can I praise a citizen who's willful, and who treats his fellow townsmen harshly, out of narrow-mindedness.

My case is different. Unexpected trouble has crushed my soul. It's over now; I take no joy in life. My friends, I want to die. My husband, who was everything to me— how well I know it—is the worst of men.

Of all the living creatures with a soul and mind, we women are the most pathetic[①].

---

① pathetic: adj. 可怜的，悲惨的

First of all, we have to buy a husband: spend vast amounts of money, just to get a master for our body—to add insult to injury[①]. And the stakes could not be higher: will you get a decent husband, or a bad one? If a woman leaves her husband, then she loses her virtuous reputation. To refuse him is just not possible. When a girl leaves home and comes to live with new ways, different rules, she has to be a prophet[②]—learn somehow the art of dealing smoothly with her bedmate. If we do well, and if our husbands bear the yoke[③] without discomfort or complaint, our lives are admired. If not, it's best to die. A man, when he gets fed up with the people at home, can go elsewhere to ease his heart—he has friends, companions his own age. We must rely on just one single soul. They

---

① add insult to injury: 雪上加霜
② prophet: n. 先知
③ yoke: n. 羁绊

say that we lead safe, untroubled lives at home while they do battle with the spear. They're wrong. I'd rather take my stand behind a shield three times than go through childbirth once.

Still, my account is quite distinct from yours. This is your city. You have your fathers' homes your lives bring joy and profit. You have friend But I have been deserted and outraged—left without a city by my husband, who stole me as his plunder① from the land of the barbarians. Here I have no mother, no brother, no blood relative to help unmoor② me from this terrible disaster.

So, I will need to ask you one small favor. If I should find some way, some strategy to pay my husband back, bring him to justice, keep silent. Most of the time, I know, a woman is filled with fear. She's

---

① plunder: n. 抢夺，掠夺的财物
② unmoor: v. 起锚，解缆

worthless in a battle and fiinches① at the sight of steel. But when she's faced with an injustice in the bedroom, there is no other mind more murderous.

——Euripides

啊,你们科任托斯妇女,我害怕你们见怪,已从屋里出来了。我知道,有许多人因为态度好像很傲慢,就得到了恶意和冷淡的骂名,他们当中有一些倒也出来跟大家见面,可是一般人的眼光不可靠,他们没有看清楚一个人的内心,便对那人的外表发生反感,其实那人对他们并没有什么恶意呢;还有许多则是因为他们安安静静呆在家里。一个外邦人应同本地人亲密来往;我可不赞成那种本地人,他们只求个人的享乐,不懂得社交礼貌,很惹人讨厌。

但是,朋友们,我碰见了一件意外的事,精神上受到了很大的打击。我几经完了,我宁愿死掉,这生命已没有一

---

① flinch:v. 退缩,畏惧

点乐趣。我那丈夫，我一生的幸福所依靠的丈夫，已变成这人间最恶的人！

在一切有理智、有灵性的生物当中，我们女人算是最不幸的。首先，我们得用重金争购一个丈夫，他反会变成我们的主人；但是，如果不去购买丈夫，那又是更可悲的事。而最重要的后果还要看我们得到的，是一个好丈夫，还是一个坏家伙。因为离婚对于我们女人是不名誉的事，我们又不能把我们的丈夫轰出去。一个在家里什么都不懂的女子，走进一种新的习惯和风俗里面，得变作一个先知，知道怎样驾驭她的丈夫。如果这事做得很成功，我们的丈夫接受婚姻的羁绊，那么，我们的生活便是可羡的；要不然，我们还是死了好。

一个男人同家里的人住得烦恼了，可以到外面去散散他的心里的郁积，不是找朋友，就是找玩耍的人；可是我们女人就只能靠着一个人。他们男人反说我们安处在家中，全然没有生命危险；他们却要拿着长矛上阵：这说法真是荒谬。我宁愿提着盾牌打三次仗，也不愿

生一次孩子。

可是同样的话,不能应用在你们身上:这是你们的城邦,你们的家乡,你们有丰富的生活,有朋友来往;我却孤孤单单在此流落,那家伙把我从外地抢来,又这样将我虐待,我没有母亲、弟兄、亲戚,不能逃出这灾难,到别处去停泊。

我只求你们这样帮助我:要是我想出了什么方法、计策去向我的丈夫,向那嫁女的国王和新婚的公主寻求报复,请替我保守秘密。女人总是什么都害怕,走上战场,看见刀兵,总是心惊胆战;可是受了丈夫欺负的时候,就没有别的心比她更毒辣!

作者:欧里庇得斯(古希腊公元前485或480~公元前406)

出处:《美狄亚》

背景:欧里庇得斯与埃斯库罗斯和索福克勒斯并称为希腊三大悲剧大师,他一生共创作了九十多部作品,保留至今的有十八部。他对宗教信仰持怀疑态度,责怪神明对人残忍。他注意写实,写普通人，甚至把神话中的英雄也当作普通人来描写，因而他表现的悲剧标志着传统英雄悲剧的终结和向世态戏剧的过渡。《美狄亚》批判不合理的婚姻制度和男女地位的不平等，痛责男子的不道德和自私自利。

# 跋

## 可给人些许启迪的书

**李肇星**

人类历史长河中,东西方文化、南北方文化各具特色、相互作用,构成了全世界共同的精神财富。为了中华民族的和平发展和伟大复兴,我们需要悉心借鉴优秀外国文化。幸运的是,国外经典浩如烟海,不缺乏值得看的东西;可惜的是,国内的经典都无法尽读,哪有时间和精力去遨游国外书海呢?于是,译点国外经典名言佳句就顺应人心和时代要求了。

莎士比亚说过,"书籍是全世界的营养品"。《译点经典》这本书采撷虽少如大洋滴水,却不失为厚积薄发,智慧浓缩,营养价值较高。读者一旦开卷,便可能爱不释手,数分钟内就随处可见名山巨川、古迹名胜、深林幽谷、奇葩异卉……韵味无穷,于身于心都有益处。

全书中、英文对照，译文尽可能选信、达、雅相济的，这有利于拉近读者同国外经典的距离，也可为英语学习者提供一点课外泛读材料。

饱览经典非一日之功，贵在勤学多思，触类旁通。

当代大学者王蒙引用过旧时代中国北方农村一句"经典"："下雨天打孩子——闲着也是闲着"。不妨在第一时间就打开这本小书先扫两眼。再忙，总有下雨下雪的时候，总能每星期抽出半个小时吧——这半个小时可能引你入胜，为你展现一个新的精神境界。

不久前，基辛格博士把他一本六百页的新著赠给我时调侃道：李，这书并不伟大，但你要是能看完，定会成为伟大的读者（a great reader）。我心里笑，我怕难以从头到尾（from cover to cover）读完，但会仔细阅读我关注的部分，便说：我将争取当半个或四分之一个"伟大读者"。那"伟大作者"高兴了，说他也是忙里偷闲，有选择地阅读。

没办法，现代人忙，而应读的书比古

人多，何况还要读报刊、函电、E-mail……为寻找适当的阅读方法，这本书也可给人些许启迪。

**2010年1月8日北京宁波途中**

读书笔记

读书笔记

读书笔记